Tinsl Presents

Can You Catch Santa?

Inspired by True Events

By

Kody Evans

For my son, Hunter

You've inspired my life.

Table of Contents

Chapter One
Christmas Past..1

Chapter Two
Christmas Present..12

Chapter Three
Rebel Without a Claus..20

Chapter Four
Believe in Your Elf...29

Chapter Five
Sleigh What?!..36

Chapter One

Christmas Past

All stories have to begin somewhere, and mine starts in my school newsroom.

My name is Hunter, and I am a fourth grader at Pacific Cascades Elementary. It was a Thursday in early December, and as the school reporter, I was busy thinking about my next article. This wasn't just any story. This was the *biggest* story of my career, and it had fallen right into my lap, or should I say, right into my living room.

It all started last Christmas. You see, I had woken up in the middle of the night with a dry throat, and if I'm being honest, a sneaky plan to check and see what presents were under the tree before my parents woke up. With quiet, careful footsteps, I headed down the stairs to get a drink and rattle a box or two. The house was dark, really dark, and so quiet. Although I passed many light switches on my way down the stairs, I left them all turned off. I was worried that turning the lights on might wake my parents. A quick look to see if Santa had come and something to drink was all that I needed. Using my hands to slowly guide me down the stairs, I found my way into the kitchen and poured myself a drink. Our cat, Cabbage, was asleep on the counter. He opened a single blue eye, yawned, and went straight back to sleep.

It was then I looked towards the brightly lit tree and spotted the presents. I could also see my stocking was full. Excited, I set my cup down, but when the glass hit the counter, it made a very loud sound, and that's the moment my crazy story really began.

In the darkness of the living room, a streak of bright crimson red darted right before me. Too fast to follow, it flashed to the tree, then to the plate of cookies, back to the fireplace, and in the blink of an eye, disappeared. It all happened so fast I could barely believe my eyes, and my whole body was tingling. It couldn't be. It was impossible. The evidence was right in front of my eyes, on the plate of cookies, that was now just a plate of crumbs.

I'd just *seen* Santa!

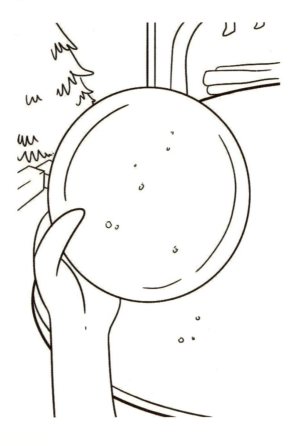

Back at school, after winter break, I waited the entire morning to share my story. As lunch approached, my excitement grew, and I jogged to the cafeteria thinking about what my friends might say once they heard my news. I'd only taken a few steps inside when I noticed that one of my friends, Lily, was standing at the table with her arms crossed. Her face was bright red and her lip was trembling. As I got closer, she brushed past me crying, "It's true, I did see him!" And with that, she stomped outside into the playground.

It didn't seem like a good time to share my story, so I sat quietly and unpacked my lunch. The rest of the kids began talking about how Lily liked to make things up. Nervously I asked, "Make up what kind of things?"

Toby, a boy sitting next to me said, "Santa. She said she caught him zipping around her house like a tornado!" The entire table burst into laughter, with Toby slapping his thigh just like my grandpa sometimes liked to. My teeth bit into the crust of my sandwich, but I wasn't that hungry anymore. As the kids teased Lily, my stomach began to twist and turn, but instead of saying that they were wrong and that I had seen Santa just like she had— I stuffed my mouth and remained quiet.

Later that day, I waited for the bus and saw Lily standing alone by the trees. She looked sad, so I waved and smiled, but she hardly looked at me. I couldn't help but wonder how I might feel if I were in her shoes. If I'd just made it to lunch a little faster, everyone would be laughing at me now. Besides, could I really be certain that I had seen Santa? The Christmas tree lights had been flashing, and my eyes had been filled with sleep. Maybe the kids were right, and we were silly to think we'd really seen Santa.

Chapter Two

Christmas Present

As the year passed, I forgot all about my Christmas secret, and instead I focused on finding stories for the school paper. There was a story about Mrs. Watkins's dog, who could walk on its hind legs, and a big scandal about the new pineapple Jell-O in the cafeteria. As I shared each new story, there was always a small but terrible feeling that I was ignoring the biggest story of all.

As December approached, *he* began to appear more often, until I couldn't go anywhere without seeing him. There was the big, inflatable Santa on my neighbor's roof. The Christmas cards with Santa's jolly face and snowy white beard. Santa was in Christmas movies, TV commercials, and shop windows, always laughing at me with his booming

Ho,Ho,Ho!

Christmas was only one week away when I finally decided I'd had enough. My class had an afternoon study period, so I sat down and began writing a whole new story—the story I should have written a year earlier, but had been too embarrassed to. For an hour my pen scribbled across the page, and I was halfway through describing the empty plate of cookies when *Whoosh!* A big gust of wind and snow blew the window beside me open, sending paper and pens flying. I jumped out of my chair and quickly closed it, with my eyes fixed on the swirling white shapes just beyond the glass.

I joined the other kids in class to pick up all the objects that had blown around the room and returned to my article. When I finally sat down, I saw that a new item had appeared on my desk. At first, I thought someone had misplaced it, but then I noticed the large looping writing that spelled out my name: HUNTER.

The letter had no sender. The paper was thick and seemed to be hand-written. I looked at it for a while, my stomach began to twist in knots. It smelled like pine and fresh snow, and it made me feel nervous and excited, all at once. Telling myself I was being silly, I decided it must be a Christmas message from one of my friends. I carefully picked up the soft, heavy paper. It almost seemed to unfold itself, falling open in my hands. There was only a very short message written in the same big swooping letters. I smoothed my hand across the folds to flatten it out as best as I could. With my eyes locked on the page, my lips whispered the strange, mysterious words.

"Can you catch Santa?"

With wonder, I read those four words again and again. I didn't know if it was a prank or if it was for real. Had someone peeked over my shoulder and seen the article I'd been writing a moment before? I glanced over at Lily, who was at the table beside me. It was hard to believe any kid could draw such fancy letters, and besides, Lily had no reason to give that letter to me. She must have felt me looking at her because she glanced up, blushed, and then looked back down at her book. I sat with that heavy paper gripped in my hand for what felt like hours . . . until the class bell rang and it was time to go home.

That night I moved the food around on my dinner plate, but when my mom asked what was wrong, I only shrugged. If I told them the truth, they'd probably think I was crazy! That night I sat at my desk and knew what I had to do. There was a mystery to be solved, and I was a reporter. The time to sit and worry was over. Picking up the article I'd started that afternoon, I put pen to paper and began to write.

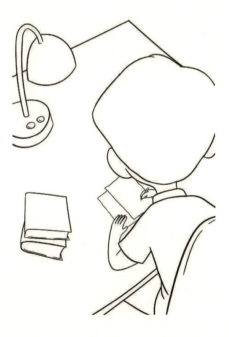

Chapter Three

REBEL WITHOUT A CLAUS

The article was titled "Can You Catch Santa?" It included all the different stories I'd heard from friends and family over the years: the cookies and milk that disappeared, footprints left in living rooms, and sleigh bells that jingled in the middle of the night. I ended the article with the most exciting evidence of all, my own sighting of Santa, the Christmas before. The article finished with a request to my readers to *Please, send your ideas on how to catch Santa. Serious suggestions only!* As I typed those final words, my shoulders felt a bit lighter, and I hoped Lily wouldn't be too upset at me for keeping my silence back in third grade. Now it would all be out in the open. I had seen Santa, and this year I was going to catch him. I was sure plenty of kids had tried—and failed—in the past. I would be the first to succeed.

My original plan involved setting up some sort of a trap to capture him in my home, but I quickly realized that would leave thousands of children without presents, and likely land me on the naughty list forever. All I wanted was a piece of evidence that would prove once and for all that Lily and I had told the truth, but I was running out of time.

In the last week of school, my story was published and it created quite a buzz. The school secretary even delivered a huge pile of letters to my class, including long lists of ideas to catch Santa. With a beating heart, I checked to see if any of the notes were written on that same soft, thick paper, but my mysterious pen pal had remained silent.

Hoping for a great idea, I looked through the letters but found that all the suggestions were too obvious. Santa was far too clever to fall for a giant cookie that would take an hour to eat, or a large net at the end of the chimney. With a heavy heart, I began winter break with a whole lot of questions, and almost zero answers. Christmas was only a few sleeps away and time was running out. My eyes were down at my feet as I trudged up the porch steps and lifted my hand to open the door. It was here that I paused at the small red sticker just above the doorknob. It had a picture of a camera with the letters *CCTV*.

Aha, that was it!

In a rush of breath, the plan popped right into my head. Our home had video cameras at the front of the house, and in the gardens. We had baby cameras, tablet cameras, phone cameras . . . a dozen invisible eyes to catch Santa in the act. In fact, we might have caught him already! I was wild-eyed as I exploded into the kitchen to ask my mom if I could see the videos from Christmas Eve, the year before.

She gave me a strange look, and for a moment I was sure she'd say no, but then she agreed.

Sitting down with both my mom and dad, we went through every recording. I saw the doorbell recordings of all of the family coming on Christmas morning, my baby brother crying on his crib monitor, and snow falling on our security cameras. There were hours of footage, but no sign of Santa. With a sigh, I remembered that the red flash I'd seen had moved towards the chimney, and we didn't have a camera in the garden that caught that angle. I thanked my parents for letting me look through the recordings and stomped off to my room. Not long after, my dad walked in and asked, "What's going on, Pal?"

I rubbed my eyes, feeling the start of a headache. "Have you ever tried to capture Santa, Dad?"

He replied, "When I was a kid, I tried to stay up too many times to count. Sometimes I wondered if he had a special kind of sleeping spell, because I could never keep my eyes open."

It was then that I let out my big secret. I had seen Santa, and not only that, I'd now written an article in the school paper, promising to catch Santa once and for all. But, what if I failed? Just like Lily, I'd be the school joke.

Dad tried to make me feel better, but he didn't understand. Santa was too fast to be filmed on camera, zipping from house to house. No one had caught him before, so how did I have any chance? "You're a great reporter," my dad said, ruffling my hair. "You'll figure it out."

That night in bed, my thoughts swirled like the white snow outside my window. I tried to sleep, but all I could see were the laughing faces of my school friends, pointing and whispering. As my chest grew tighter, I realized there were a couple of places that Santa didn't move quite as quickly, which explained how I'd managed to see him in the first place. Zipping up and down chimneys was one thing, but eating cookies, drinking milk, and filling stockings took a little more time. Lying in the dark, my mind schemed with possibilities.

The plan was simple.

Chapter Four

BELIEVE IN YOUR ELF

Step 1: Whoopee Cushion

When Santa came down the chimney, he'd get a loud surprise. My whoopee cushion was loud enough to wake the neighbors, and when Santa landed on it, no amount of speed would stop him from announcing his arrival. While I crept downstairs, he would be further distracted once he noticed something different about the stockings. .

Step 2: The Extra Stocking

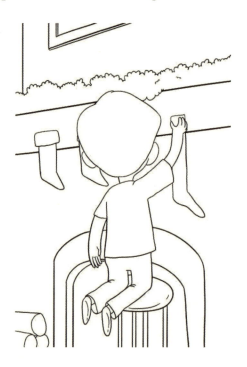

Everyone knew Santa kept a careful list of all the children in the world, and the presents on their wish lists. Discovering an extra stocking would force him to pull out his list to check who his elves might have missed.

Step 3: The Double-Iced Cookie

Every year Mom bakes delicious ginger cookies for Santa to munch on, but this year, the icing would be on both sides, gluing the cookie to the plate. With his list in one hand and a cookie in the other, Santa would be stuck as I snuck closer with my interview questions, ready to finally get answers to all those mysterious Christmas questions. Is Rudolph's nose really red? What do Christmas elves like to eat, exactly? A good reporter would simply try to catch Santa in the act. I was a *great* reporter, and I was going to get the scoop of a lifetime.

Step 4: The Recording

Every reporter knows that sometimes you have to use the latest gadgets, so I asked my dad if he could download an app onto his phone that would only start recording if it detected movement. I would set up the phone in a plant beside the kitchen table, where we usually left the milk and cookies. I would also place a letter beside the glass of milk, because I thought Santa might pause for even longer if he had something to read.

With all the steps worked out, I finally relaxed into a deep sleep. There was no way Santa would be able to wriggle through all the traps I had planned.

As I counted down the last days to Christmas, I could barely sit still. I thought through the steps in my plan, did a few experiments (it turned out the whoopee cushion needed to be on something soft, like a towel, so that it didn't slip) and practiced tiptoeing downstairs, as quiet as our cat, Cabbage.

When Christmas Eve finally arrived, I set up every part of my grand plan and laid in bed staring at the clock. Morning was still hours away and sleep seemed impossible. It had been a big couple of weeks for me and eventually the numbers on the clock began to blur. My eyelids slowly drooped lower and…

FRRRRRRRPPPPP!

I opened my eyes and blinked into the dark. There was only one possible explanation for that sound! As quietly and as quickly as I could, I threw back the covers, grabbed my interview questions, and tiptoed down the stairs. This was the moment I had worked so hard for. I imagined seeing Santa standing in the living room, with one hand on a cookie, and the other on his list, unaware that he was about to give his first real interview, ever. I glided down the hallway and sped up once I spotted a new present under the tree. He'd visited! But, was he still inside the house?

Chapter Five

SLEIGH WHAT?!

Running, I almost tripped over our cat, Cabbage, who meowed in annoyance and darted down the hall. As soon as I reached the kitchen, I spun around searching every corner . . . but the room was empty. I let my list of interview questions drop to the floor, but I wasn't too disappointed. As expected, the plate of cookies was now a plate with crumbs and the last bits of icing. The milk was gone, and the extra stocking remained empty. I checked the whoopee cushion hidden at the bottom of the chimney and found all the air squished out of it, but the best clue of all was waiting in the plant beside the kitchen table. My dad's phone sat still and silent, waiting to reveal its secrets. From what I could see, I'd definitely slowed Santa down—but had I missed my chance?

A loud thump from the doorway had me jumping out of my skin, but it was only my mom and dad, rubbing at their eyes and asking if everything was okay. "I think I did it!" I said, as I grabbed the phone. "I think I filmed Santa!"

My dad reached out and I reluctantly handed over the phone, looking over his arm as he opened up the video recording app. His big, bushy eyebrows came together. "There is a new recording," he said in his deep, croaky voice. I tried to hide my excitement, but I simply couldn't. We all sat around watching the video. The camera was focused on the full plate of cookies and the glass of milk. Cabbage—my greedy cat—was standing on the table trying to stick his face in the glass, his small, pink tongue darting at the milk. "Cabbage!" I hissed, hoping he was ashamed of himself. "That milk was for Santa!" Cabbage's movements must have started the recording.

I began to wonder if maybe Santa had beat me once again, when a loud *FRRRRRRRPPPPP* erupted from the phone's speaker, and onscreen,

Cabbage leapt off the table. I turned to my mom and dad, whose eyes were even wider than mine.

"Did Cabbage toot?" asked my dad, but I waved him away and said I'd explain later.

Then, on the video, I saw a flash of red. It could have been a weird shadow from one of the Christmas lights, but I knew better. "There he is!" I screamed. My mom flinched, covering her ear. "Sorry, Mom!"

This was the big moment. I waited for Santa to stop in front of the table, ready to finally see his jolly red cheeks and laughing eyes as he wrestled with the cookies. Just like that, a big white face with bright blue eyes filled the screen. Except it wasn't Santa . . .

"Cabbage!"

My annoying, fluffy cat sniffed at the camera for a moment, before hopping back out of the frame with a short, grumpy meow. A moment later, I ran into the frame, tripping over Cabbage and gasping in excitement as I spotted the empty plate of cookies. It was hard to see the joy in my face. I'd been so sure I would catch him, but in the end, I'd been outwitted by a four-legged fiend.

"You're a bad cat!" I yelled down the hall.

My dad reached out his hand and placed it on my shoulder. "Maybe next year."

I slumped. "Thought it'd work."

"It did," my dad replied, "but Santa has been sneaking in and out of houses for hundreds of years. You almost got him, but he got a lucky break. I'm sure you got closer than anyone else."

"What about my article?" I said, feeling a familiar heaviness begin to pool in my chest.

Mom put her arm around my shoulders and gave a little squeeze. She asked, "What's the most important job of a good reporter?"

"Having a good pen." That was easy. No one wanted to be halfway through an interview and run out of ink.

She laughed. "And?"

I frowned, thinking hard. "Telling the truth."

"Exactly." She rubbed her hand up and down my back, as she always did when she wanted to make me feel better. "You have a great story to tell. It might not be the one you wanted, but it's the truth," she said. "Sometimes, trying to solve the mystery is just as much fun as finding the answer." I nodded, and she stood up. "Let's clean up, and then we can open our presents."

Mom was right. Half the fun of Santa was trying to catch him. Santa was magical after all, and magic can't be trapped, or interviewed, or explained. It just *is*.

Lost in thought, I reached down and grabbed the empty glass of milk, and the plate beside it. As I lifted the glass, I noticed a piece of paper underneath, neatly folded, with the name HUNTER spelled in large looping letters.

"No way," I whispered.

With my heart in my throat, I picked it up and noticed my hand was shaking. I could hear mom and dad behind me, moving around the kitchen, but I might as well have been in an empty house. The whole world went silent and narrowed down to the small white square in my hands. I unfolded the paper, half afraid, and half excited out of my mind. The words inside were big, bold, and seemed to ring with laughter.

"Can You Catch Me?"

Santa was generous, jolly, and the very heart of what made Christmas special. It turned out he was also pretty cheeky.

"Challenge accepted," I said, folding the paper and slipping it in my pocket.

When the break was over, everyone was eager to know if I had lived up to my promise to catch

Santa. Some people laughed; others whispered that they too had seen Santa over the years. For once, none of that really mattered to me. I kept my lips sealed and told them they'd have to pick up the next edition of the school paper to get the story.

When the paper was printed, every copy had disappeared from the library by lunchtime. The school secretary said that it was a new record. I walked through the cafeteria, past a sea of faces that were tucked into the black and white pages. The headline: *"Watch Out, Santa"* seemed to have grabbed their attention. Some people were chuckling, and one girl even said "Cabbage, you're a bad cat!"

In the distance I spotted Lily, who had a copy of the newspaper lying beside her lunch tray. When I sat down beside her, I half expected her to yell at me for taking so long to tell the truth.

Instead, she smiled. "Did he smell like pine needles to you, too?"

I scrunched my nose, thinking back to the night he'd rushed right past me. "Yeah. Pine needles, fresh snow, and perhaps a hint of sugar."

She nodded. "All the cookies," she said, before telling me more about her own adventures chasing Santa.

In the end, I realized that it didn't really matter whether you'd seen Santa, or thought that people who had were silly, or lying. What mattered most was being true to what Santa meant to you. For

Lily, Santa Claus was someone she dreamed of meeting one day, perhaps while visiting his magical toy workshop in the North Pole. For me, he was a challenge and a quest: the story of the year.

What Santa means to you . . . well, that's up to you.

You might have one last question for me, and I think I know what it is. Will I try again next year? WITHOUT A DOUBT . . . and next year, Cabbage will be upstairs with me!

Watch out, Santa!